# Meet my neighbor, the doctor

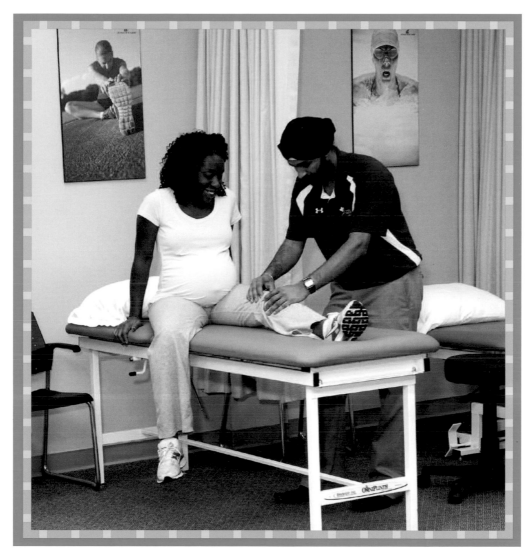

## Marc Crabtree

### Author and Photographer

Crabtree Publishing Company

www.crabtreebooks.com

# Crabtree Publishing Company

## Meet my neighbor, the doctor

For Ravi Ahluwalia, with thanks

**Author and photographer**
Marc Crabtree

**Editorial director**
Kathy Middleton

**Editor**
Reagan Miller

**Proofreader**
Crystal Sikkens

**Design**
Samantha Crabtree

**Production coordinator and prepress technician**
Ken Wright

**Print coordinator**
Katherine Berti

**Photographs**
All photographs by Marc Crabtree except:
Shutterstock: pages 3, 24 (except checkup)

**Library and Archives Canada Cataloguing in Publication**

Crabtree, Marc
    Meet my neighbor, the doctor / Marc Crabtree, author and photographer.

(Meet my neighbor)
ISBN 978-0-7787-0871-1 (bound).--ISBN 978-0-7787-0875-9 (pbk.)

    1. Ahluwalia, Ravi, 19??- --Juvenile literature.  2. Doctors--Canada--Biography--Juvenile literature.  3. Doctors--Juvenile literature.  I. Title.
IV. Series: Crabtree, Marc.  Meet my neighbor.

RK43.M43C73 2010          j617.6092          C2009-906758-7

**Library of Congress Cataloging-in-Publication Data**

CIP available at Library of Congress

## Crabtree Publishing Company

Printed in Canada/012013/MA20121217

www.crabtreebooks.com          1-800-387-7650

**Published in Canada**
**Crabtree Publishing**
616 Welland Ave.
St. Catharines, Ontario
L2M 5V6

**Published in the United States**
**Crabtree Publishing**
PMB 59051
350 Fifth Avenue, 59th Floor
New York, New York 10118

**Published in the United Kingdom**
**Crabtree Publishing**
Maritime House
Basin Road North, Hove
BN41 1WR

**Published in Australia**
**Crabtree Publishing**
3 Charles Street
Coburg North
VIC, 3058

# Contents

Meet my Neighbor

Meet my neighbor Ravi Ahluwalia. Ravi is a doctor.

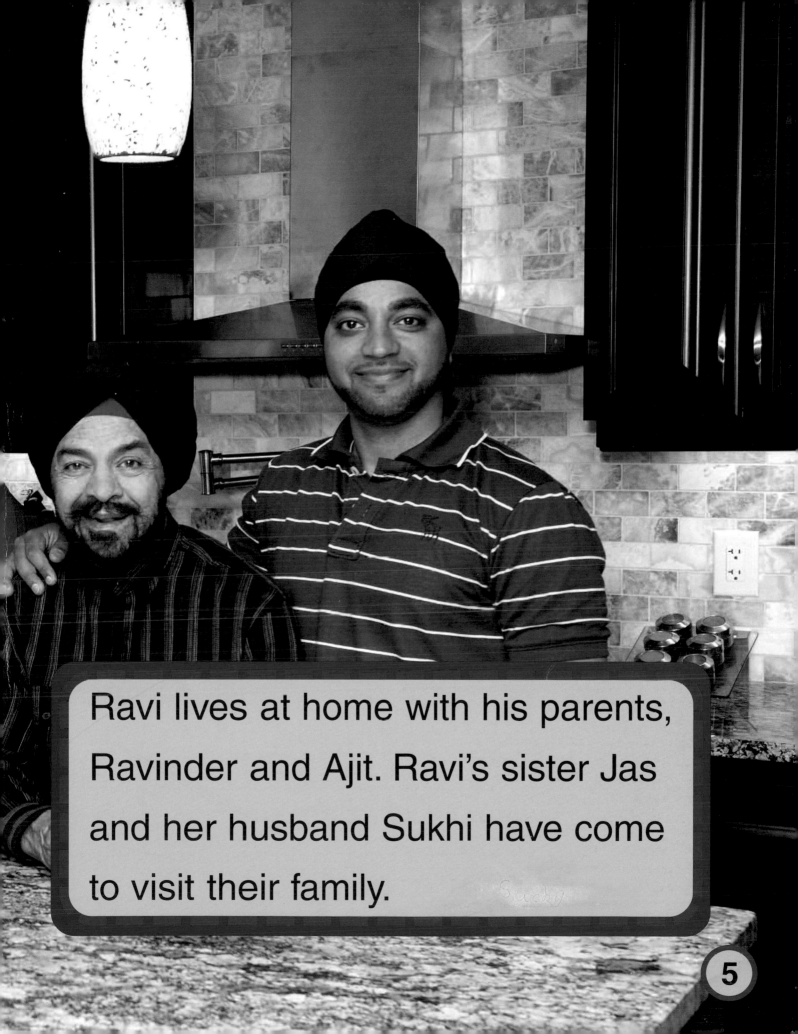

Ravi lives at home with his parents, Ravinder and Ajit. Ravi's sister Jas and her husband Sukhi have come to visit their family.

Ravi works at a family health clinic. He cares for adults and children that are hurt or sick. The people he cares for are called patients. Ravi helps keep his patients healthy.

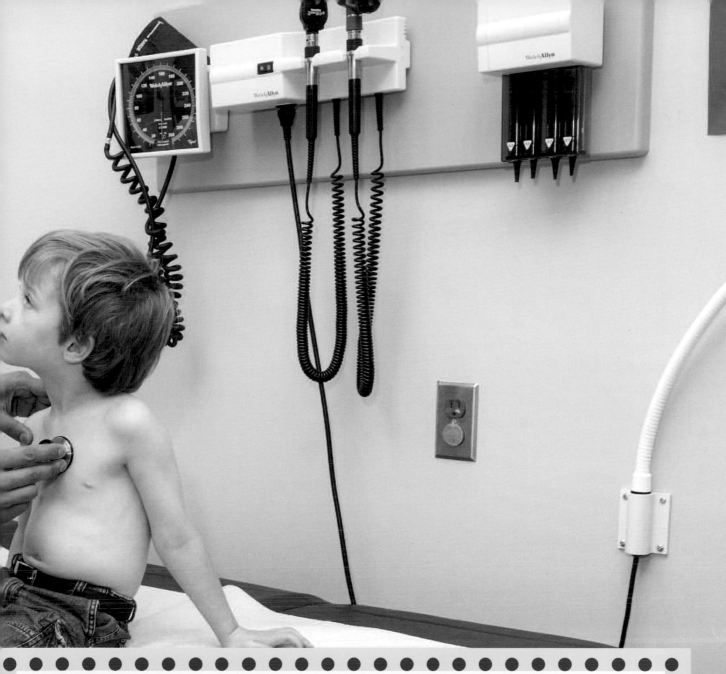

Ravi starts his day by giving his patient Dexter a **checkup**. Ravi uses a tool called a **stethoscope** to listen to Dexter's heartbeat. Ravi wants to make sure Dexter's body is healthy.

Ravi's next patient is a little girl named Bonnie. Bonnie has an earache. Ravi uses an **otoscope** to look inside Bonnie's ears. He gives Bonnie medicine to help her ear feel better.

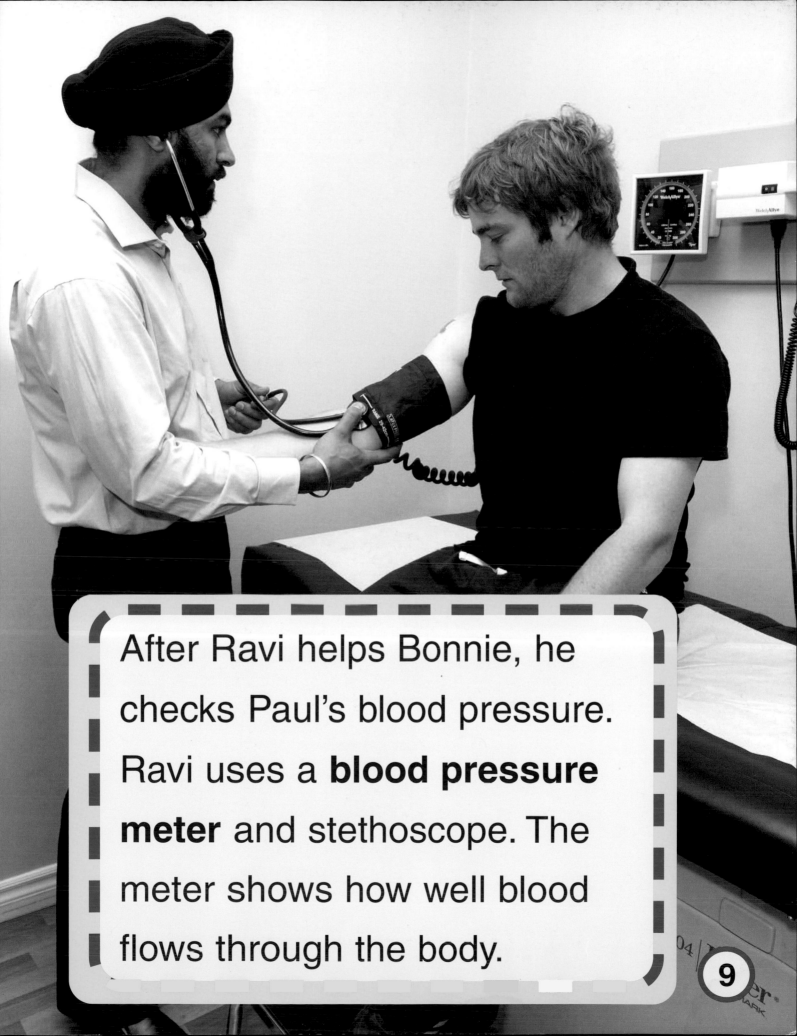

After Ravi helps Bonnie, he checks Paul's blood pressure. Ravi uses a **blood pressure meter** and stethoscope. The meter shows how well blood flows through the body.

Nurses work at the family health clinic, too. Doctors and nurses work together as a team to help people stay healthy. The nurses at the clinic help Ravi care for the patients.

Ravi's next patient has cut his hand. The man needs stitches to close the cut. Ravi stitches up the cut and covers it with a bandage to help it heal.

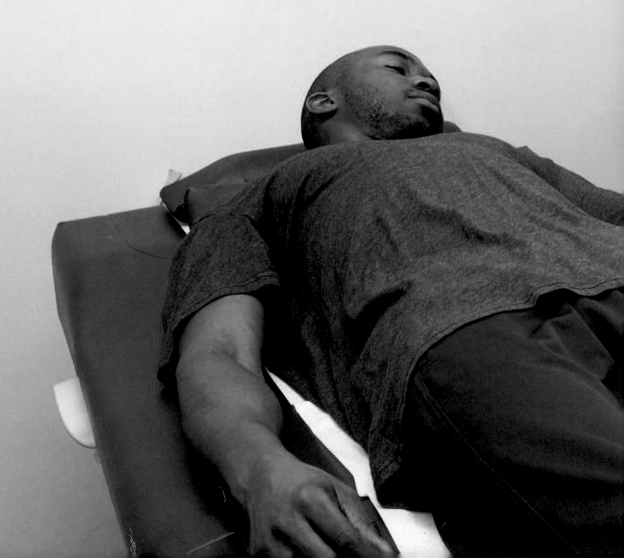

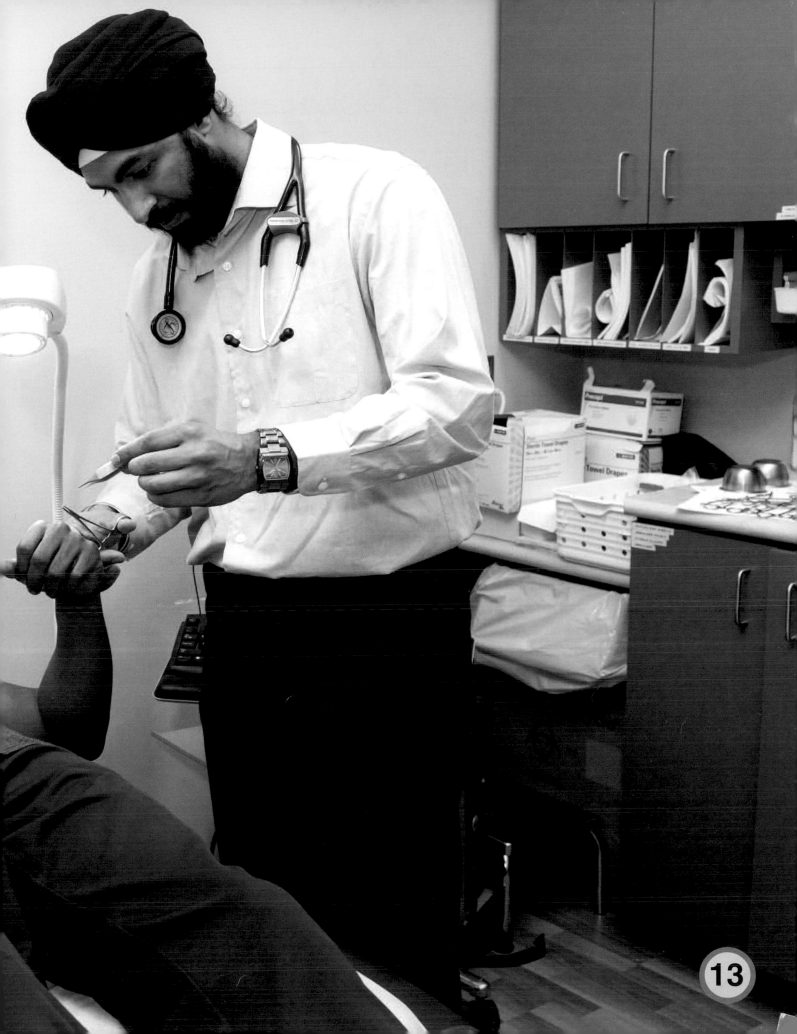

Ravi also works at a sports therapy clinic. At this clinic, Ravi cares for people who have hurt themselves while exercising or playing sports.

Ravi's patient Natalie is recovering from a sports injury. He suggests she use a **stationary bike** to help her muscles get stronger.

Using weights will also help heal Natalie's injury faster. Ravi is showing Natalie some exercises she can do.

Ravi's next patient is Jennifer. She has hurt her knee while exercising. Ravi uses a **reflex hammer** to test Jennifer's reflexes.

A reflex hammer is one tool that Ravi uses to help him find out what is wrong with his patients.

An X-ray is another tool Ravi uses. An X-ray is a photograph or picture of the inside of a person's body.

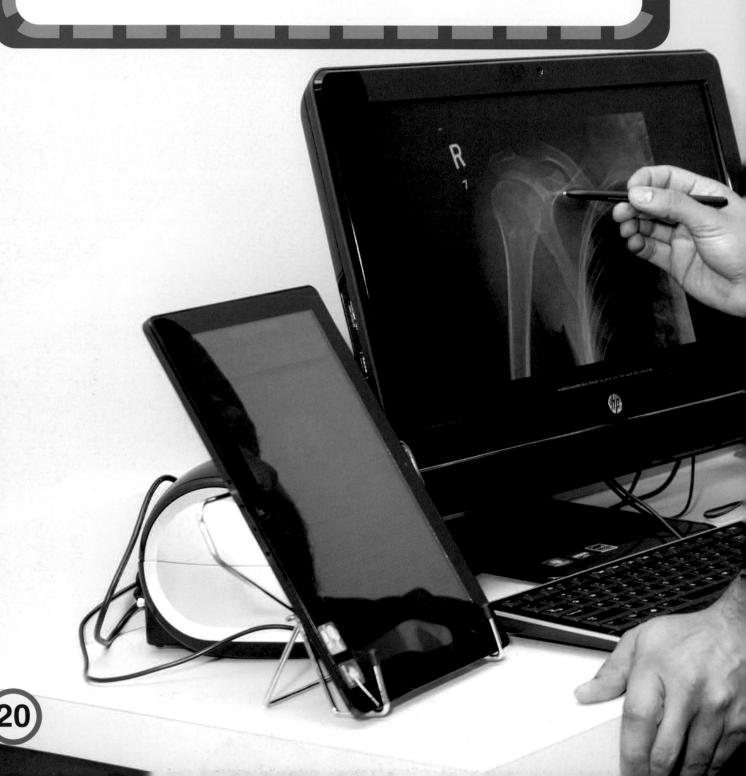

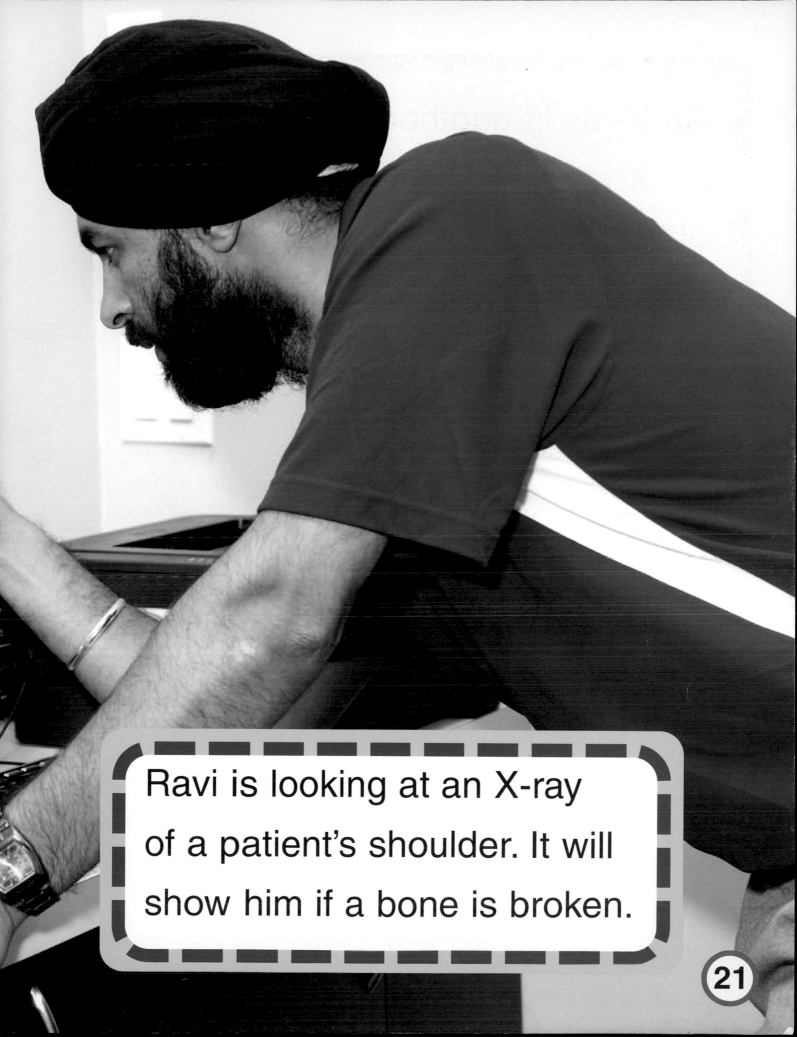

Ravi is looking at an X-ray of a patient's shoulder. It will show him if a bone is broken.

Ravi also works as a sports team doctor. He goes to games and cares for any athletes that get hurt.

This soccer player hurt his leg. It is a good thing Ravi is there to help! He wraps the player's leg with a bandage.

23

# Glossary

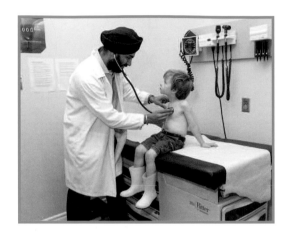

checkup

stethoscope

otoscope

blood pressure meter

stationary bike

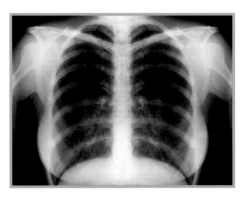

X-ray

reflex hammer